THE BRAND ADVOCATE

THE BRAND ADVOCATE

A Strategy-Driven Workbook

Bill Nissim

iUniverse, Inc.

New York Lincoln Shanghai

The Brand Advocate

A Strategy-Driven Workbook

Copyright © 2005 by William H. Nissim

iUniverse books may be ordered through booksellers or by contacting:

iUniverse
2021 Pine Lake Road, Suite 100
Lincoln, NE 68512
www.iuniverse.com
1-800-Authors (1-800-288-4677)

ISBN-13: 978-0-595-37619-3 (pbk)
ISBN-13: 978-0-595-82011-5 (ebk)
ISBN-10: 0-595-37619-3 (pbk)
ISBN-10: 0-595-82011-5 (ebk)

Printed in the United States of America

This book is dedicated to my lovely wife. Her graceful approach and impeccable insights gave pause to my musings and inspired greater clarity of thought. I am forever grateful for her patience, support, and wisdom.

CONTENTS

▼

Introduction

Who is the advocate for your organization's most valuable asset? Is that you?

How compelling is your brand story? If I said Hershey's ^{TM}, do you think "chocolate"? Is Fed-X ^{TM} synonymous with overnight parcel delivery? In your mind, does Starbucks ^{TM} = coffee. Can you say the same about your organization?

These examples plainly demonstrate a simple, yet clear value proposition. Your ability to instantly make these types of associations illustrates a powerful brand strategy at work. Someone in each of these notable firms became the Brand Advocate who gave life and meaning to their product or service. Without a clear and compelling Brand Strategy, the ability to reach both the minds and hearts of your targeted audience will falter.

So, how do you become a Brand Advocate?

This workbook will transform the way you think about branding! In each chapter, it discusses the essentials of branding and then invokes the reader to reflect on their current situation. Most importantly, it compels the reader to actively respond to those questions using an interactive approach. The final chapter summarizes answers taken from each section and then creates a roadmap for a successful brand strategy. By working through this process, you will become the advocate for your brand.

What drove me to write this workbook? First, it became evident that a practical branding workbook was not commercially available. Many branding books present concepts and case studies; they provide great insights, but they leave it up to the reader to discern key points and more importantly, don't explain how to apply those ideas. The Brand Advocate will walk the marketing practitioner through the process.

Secondly, I have a personal passion for branding and recognized early on its strategic value. As a result, I've taken my accumulated professional experience and education in this field and condensed it into building blocks that can help you create a powerful brand strategy for your organization. I strongly feel that the fuel of business is the organization and its financial performance, but the engine is the brand itself. Top management would be well served to embrace and elevate branding to a strategic position within the organization. Conversely, those who might choose to ignore the essentials of branding may indeed suffer the consequences.

Great brands take considerable time and patience to grow and nurture. They are not the subject of single, snazzy ad campaigns. Brands also require a systematic, method-based approach to analyze, develop, and execute. This workbook guides the user through these steps and emphasizes execution.

Finally, all forms of promotion possess a tainted reputation since its very impact is uncertain. Whether you employ general advertising or direct mail, your ability to assess its effectiveness is not quantifiable. As John Wanamaker, the inventor of the department store concept once pronounced, "I know that 50% of my advertising is wasted. I just don't know which half."

Instead of measuring awareness or "share of mind," this workbook emphasizes financially based metrics to plan and measure ROI. This approach allows an organization to target opportunities; strategically fund approaches to acquiring business, and provides the metrics to analyze efforts and results. Since this process is ongoing, management can now evaluate different venues and adjust the strategy and spend to produce the most effective returns.

It is my hope that after following these essentials, your organization will enact a more effective and prudent brand strategy. After completing this workbook, you too can become a Brand Advocate!

Let's get down to Basics

Overview

After eighteen years as a marketing practitioner and having devoured most published books on the subject, it seemed to me that someone should distill the essentials of branding in a simple and concise fashion. This chapter by no means attempts to grapple with that endeavor, but merely consolidates the basics for real-world application. You may want to identify specific topics of interest and further research them to aid in your particular business situation. I'll provide three basic principles to help get you started.

Perception—Principle #1:

It was once said "perception is everything." Look around you. Everything you own, wear, and touch has meaning on a variety of different levels. The "brand" begins in your mind and directs your actions, purchases, and behavior over a lifetime. The first principle for your business begins with a brand perception. Think of McDonalds™ restaurant. Every aspect of their business adds or takes away from that organization—from the way the food tastes to the empty French-fry carton in the parking lot. Every image your organization presents to the world (from your web site to how you answer your phone) enhances or degrades how potential customers perceive your business.

<u>Value—Principle #2:</u>

What value are you providing? The best way to answer that question would be to simply look at the competition. Take time to evaluate what everyone else is doing. Find the gaps in their offerings and claim that territory as your own. The key question a potential client will ask you—what are you going to do for me today? The answer will inevitably be one of these three things: save them money, remove their pain or conflict, or make them look good (or a combination of all three!) The essential point here—to provide a value that no one else can.

<u>Differentiation—Principle #3</u>

Why do you choose Pepsi™ over Coke™, Total™ over Special K™, or Starbucks™ over Seattle's Best™? In a blind taste test, would you really know the difference? Each product exudes a combination of communication vehicles over time to assure you can tell the difference.

Trying to mimic the status quo only makes your business less distinguishable. In order to stand out from the crowd, you need to be FIRST in a category and possess a unique story to tell. The idea of a coffee house wasn't unique until Starbucks™ created the right combination of product mix, aesthetics, and messages to engender a new platform for coffee enjoyment. Until such time, the average person wouldn't dream of spending $3.50 for a cup of Joe! One final word—find a niche that hasn't been exploited and create a compelling story (perception).

BRANDING BASICS EXERCISES

Starting with principal number one, your brand doesn't reside on a label, billboard, or website—it resides in every individual's mind. This remains an area, as a business owner or leader, which you can't control. Whether you like it or not, perception rules over your product or service.

Perception may also be unfair. You may have a stellar record with your clients, and through one bad incident, you will have to spend years to trying to remove the tarnish. Remember the Exxon™ Valdez, Tylenol™ tampering, or New Coke™ incidents? On a positive note, when your clients are making key decisions between you and a newcomer, your brand value will have a compelling influence on their decision-making process.

The first step in this process is to sit back and think about your business. List FIVE descriptors that define who you are in a few words.

From your perspective, put into words a perception of what your organization is, can be, or will be in the future. This is a good start, but only the beginning of your situational analysis. Repeat the process with a colleague (don't show them your list). Compare the two. If you are an inquisitive sort, repeat this process by querying a cross-section of your organization. The more data points, the better!

Step One: <u>Your Perception</u>   Step Two: <u>Colleague's Perception</u>

1._____   _____

2._____   _____

3._____   _____

4._____   _____

5._____   _____

What's happening here? Are you finding divergent perceptions?

I first applied this method during my final year at graduate school. During the discovery phase of my Thesis, I undertook a cross-sectional brand awareness of an organization and found a wide range of responses. What management discusses in the boardroom will most likely not permeate throughout the organization without a proactive, inter-company communication program. Why are these perceptions not consistent? Even with a concerted effort, it takes time for messages to affect organizational behavior.

The importance of management and the entire organization's agreement on perception, value, and differentiation concerns how the outside world distinguishes you. For example, if you walk into a Starbucks™ and the aesthetics (building, decor, displays, and employee's attire) appear as it should, but if the employees are lazy, unfriendly, and rude, your perception of Starbucks™ shifts. If employees refuse to embrace and carry out management's values, consumers will seek another venue that addresses their needs.

As simple as it sounds, we need to ask ourselves on a daily basis why someone would want to do business with us. In the vast universe of choices, simply offering the same product or service isn't compelling enough.

Try another exercise. Please list below the extraordinary value that you bring your customers on a daily basis. Next, for each value you've listed, write down a similar value your prime competitor provides. Now, compare and contrast which values matches your customers needs and why. We will explore a "Value Gap Analysis" later in this workbook and discuss how to present that ideology to your customers.

<u>Your Organization</u>   <u>The Competition</u>

_____   _____

_____   _____

_____   _____

_____   _____

Next, let's discuss how you differentiate yourself from all other direct and indirect competitors. What does this mean? Back to the Starbucks™ business model, direct competitors might include Dietrich's ™, Seattle's Best ™, and other local coffee houses. Indirect competitors are comprised of all other venues such as Dunkin Donuts™, Winchells™, Krispy Kreme™, and even cans of coffee that line the shelves of your local grocery store.

The key to success resides in being FIRST in the minds and hearts of your audience. Differentiation helps them recognize between the two, whether directly or indirectly.

This last exercise will help you think about ways to differentiate your organization from the crowd. List five attributes where you compete on a daily basis in a DIRECT fashion. Try and stay away from price and quality and focus on aspects that your audience will really value. For example, if we are evaluating coffee houses (direct), you may note taste, aesthetics of the store, ambiance, etc. Also consider ways you compete on an indirect fashion. These are comprised of solutions that your audience may substitute in lieu of the real thing. For example, I may really desire a Venti Latte from Starbucks, but will settle (due to convenience) for a Dunkin Donuts knock-off.

Direct	Indirect
_____	_____
_____	_____
_____	_____
_____	_____
_____	_____

Now that we have covered the "basics." Let's move on to what I refer to as the essentials of branding.

Unveiling the Essentials of Branding

Overview:

During my tenure as a graduate student many years ago, the looming question on every student's mind was—what will be the locus of my research? Since my career was inundated in brand management activities, the idea of applying branding theories to a business model not readily engaged in these practices seemed challenging. As a result, an eighteen-month journey ensued to understand how an organization searches for relevance in a world of scarce resources through brand management.

To begin, a theoretical model was needed from which to view the process of branding. If you assimilate most published materials on branding, you can derive four essentials:

1. What is your overall brand perception today?
2. Describe the future brand goal?
3. Create a plan to reach that goal
4. Does the brand live throughout the organization?

Brand Perception:

An organization's greatest asset is its brand, yet so little time, energy, and care is devoted to this process and generally is relegated to a lower level functionary. In my research, the daily efforts and thin resources most organizations face yield little time for reflection. During my interviews with top management, it became apparent that brand assessment was not part of the agenda nor considered relevant. If your present brand perception is not working, step back and view it through the eyes of your potential customer. If you don't like what you see, it's time to roll up your sleeves and evaluate every facet of your brand

Brand Goal:

Defining your future brand goal is generally an easier task than looking backwards. The question that every organization should ask itself: what is the one thing that I can do better than anyone else? To be a meaningful brand, your cause must be a FIRST—a new category, approach, or service that hasn't been exploited. Since this differentiator (value proposition) sets your organization apart from all others, make sure that the organization not only believes it, but also can execute it! Once defined, every facet of the organization should be centered on that "rallying cry."

Plan:

My thesis focused on a nonprofit organization that had many competitors in a crowded market space. Their differentiator, a fully functioning village for the homeless, was groundbreaking on both a local and national level. The brand perception migrated from a decentralized rescue mission to a community that integrates a variety of functions (meals, shelter, education, behavior enhancement, hope, etc.) under one roof. This concept has the potential to become a powerful, new brand position in the local community and its attributes are easily recognizable and unique.

The next step bridges the gap between the current perception and the brand goal. As with any planning process, a series of activities that culminates into a brand shift takes time and patience. Great brands were not invented overnight and required careful planning and attention to detail. The greatest stumbling block for an organization to achieve a brand goal lies in its execution; most plans are written and then proceed to collect dust on a shelf. Brand planning requires daily attention for progression and change to occur. Also, a brand lives in the mind of each individual and has been developed through years of message layering. One Super-Bowl ad just won't cut it!

Organizational Adoption:

The key to a successful plan requires a top-down commitment and involvement. Aside from the change in external messages, a separate campaign to inform, educate, and acquire buy-in from all organizational members is essential. In order for the new brand perception to be realized, it can't be the latest management fad—it needs to reside in the hearts and minds of every single employee! My research indicated that monthly, weekly, and even daily meetings were needed to ensure a consistent message was delivered and acted upon.

ESSENTIALS EXERCISES

Brand Perception: List at least five descriptors that define your organization's perception. Unlike the exercise in the "basics" section, use terms that are emotionally based and suggest feelings evoked when thinking about your organization. For example, a child might describe McDonald's™ as fun, happy, playful, yummy, colorful, cheerful, and many others. Now think of your organization and list them in those terms:

1. _____
2. _____
3. _____
4. _____
5. _____

If you are still struggling with descriptors, maybe this example will help. I owned a BMW™ many years ago. My perception could be expressed using the following descriptors and the meaning behind them:

1. Powerful—Germanic engineering

2. Smooth—incredible suspension

3. Solid—extremely well designed and built

4. Silent—quite engine and well fitted chassis, doors, etc.

5. Luxurious—internal aesthetics and sharp chassis styling

In anyone's minds-eye, BMW™ is not about a car, torque ratios, or MPG. We associate with things that add value to our lives and have significant meaning. As selfish and self-absorbed as it may sound, we surround ourselves with brands, icons, and a myriad of images that define us. So, a person's perception of BMW™ is what it means to their life, how others will perceive them, and how it impacts their standing with friends, family, and associates. As a result, the value proposition of "The Ultimate Driving Machine" is realized through the fulfillment of those descriptors.

Looking back on your list, anyone should be able to recite at least two descriptors (five would be great!) about your organization. If you have a compelling story to tell, people will be able to pass that tribal knowledge along. Whether you feed the hungry or sell a service, people need to feel passionate about your cause or what you represent. Remember, when you see a movie that moves you to tears, it was the story line (value proposition) that wrestled with your emotions and made you feel something.

Brand Goal: We stated the brand goal was the one thing you can do better than anyone else. Please list below your future brand goal. To help you compare and contrast this objective, list your current goals for your organization on the left and what you would like them to be in the future. Remember, you must be first in a category, approach, or service to be unique.

Current Brand Goals	Future Brand Goals
_____	_____
_____	_____
_____	_____
_____	_____

What is different between your current and future brand goal? This exercise reveals your aspirations for the organization. Be mindful of a few things: this goal needs to be meaningful, attainable, and accurate. To be meaningful, it must be a cause that your organization and audience can understand and embrace. In terms of being attainable, it must possess both short and long-term milestones that the organization can reach within the confines of its resources. Finally, it must be an accurate portrayal of delivered value on a sustaining basis.

What is the acid test for a future brand goal? The example below lists the major steps your organization will need to engage in for this goal to become a reality.

1. How are we perceived today?

2. Our point of differentiation?

3. What do we aspire to be?

4. Can the organization execute that transition?

Plan: Now that you've solidified your current perception and the future brand goal, our attention shifts to building a bridge to connect the two. In the planning process, what activities should take place to affect change?

The first step is for senior management to fully embrace this paradigm shift. Once concurrence is achieved, an organizational presentation needs to be crafted that communicates this endeavor to everyone in simple, understandable terms. After this message is understood by the entire organization, monthly meetings help to engrain and exemplify the importance of this undertaking. List below the "bridges" you must create to affect change.

Current Perception   Bridge   Future Brand Goal

_____   _____   _____

_____   _____   _____

_____   _____   _____

_____   _____   _____

Organizational Adoption: The greatest challenge any organization faces is change. The idea of change is a culmination of a new understanding and behavioral modification. In addition to an educational program to implement these "bridges," a continuous commitment to live the new brand promise is critical.

People only behave according to the belief systems that are active in their environment. During my research, it was abundantly evident that the core message must reside in the hearts and minds of all employees for change to occur. This can be accomplished in one of two ways: either the employees are predisposed to a certain belief or they adopt the cause and make it personal.

Dynamic leadership (ex. Jack Welch of General Electric) provides the "rallying cry" and a means (bridge) for execution within his organization. When Jack Welch pronounced that all divisions must be FIRST or SECOND in each market they competed in, leaders had three alternatives—make it happen, sell it, or shut it down! The question is, do you have a strong, convincing, and meaningful rallying cry that your organization can embrace?

List below three possible approaches to embedding the future brand goal into the minds and hearts of your organizational members? The purpose of this exercise is to generate ideas and explore the best avenue to make your paradigm shift a reality. Another reason to explore options is that your first attempt may not be effective. Whatever venue seems suitable, the organization must be passionate about the ideology or it will fall on deaf ears.

Approach #1:_____

Approach#2:_____

Approach#3:_____

Summary: In conclusion, we examined the four essentials of branding to provide organizations with a structure from which they can reflect on their target audience. All brands should be re-evaluated continuously to assure the appropriate message and execution of goods or services is synergistic. By analyzing the present perception and projecting a future brand goal, the planning process will naturally follow. Integrating the organization in the process will be critical for the brand promise to be realized. Next, we will view the basics of marketing as it applies to branding.

Marketing: Follow the Yellow Brick Road?

When the topic of "marketing" arises in a conversation, it's always interesting to hear the numerous perceptions tied to this rather straightforward concept. The full spectrum of responses includes advertising, word-of-mouth, fluff, and my personal favorite—selling something you don't need! I believe the problem with understanding marketing resides in the over-commercialization of the term and leaves business acumen, strategy, and execution at the front door.

According to the American Marketing Association, marketing is defined as; "Marketing is the process of planning and executing the conception, pricing, promotion, and distribution of ideas, goods, and services to create exchanges that satisfy individual and organizational objectives." Sounds simple enough? If accountants follow Generally Accepted Accounting Principles (GAAP) and manufacturing managers utilize FIFO or LIFO for inventory valuation, then why does the practice of marketing not follow a similar process? Good question!

The following section is intended to be reflective in nature and prompt senior management to evaluate specific facets of their approach to marketing. I think the analogy of Dorothy's journey down the yellow brick road (Wizard of Oz fairytale) mirrors common flaws in marketing application and practice within organizations today.

To begin, all organizations have a goal or objective they want to attain. In the process of reaching that goal, they need financial supporters who hear the message and want to be part of that journey. Organizations then apply traditional marketing methods to reach those targeted supporters. Sound familiar? Dorothy, in that age-old storybook tale, had the same dilemma. To reach Emerald City and have an audience with The Wizard (to find a way home), she consulted the munchkins and mindlessly followed the yellow brick road. Let's see how this unfolds as we view the basic constructs of a plan.

Marketing Plan:

The basic problem with Dorothy's plan, as executed by most organizations, was the methodology she applied. Most plans seek traditional promotional venues to solve their immediate dilemma.

If the goal is to increase sales by 10%, most managers rush to mainstream mediums (radio, billboard, newsletters, and telemarketing) as a solution. What sounds good on paper may not actually work in practice. This unidirectional approach, sometimes called "insider mentality," delivers a stream of messages from the organization to the targeted audience with little regard for their current circumstances. Without this understanding, the channel proposed may not be suitable for the intended audience. What's the alternative?

By starting with the customer (outside-in) and their behavioral circumstances, you will effectively gain their attention, mind, and hearts. If Dorothy had asked the good witch the right question (early on), she would have known to click her heels three times and instantly returned to Kansas. In short, the yellow brick road would have become irrelevant!

When generating a marketing plan, start with your core audience and work your way back to the organization. This exercise will unveil the most direct and meaningful approach to achieving your organization's objective. You might save yourself time, energy, and valuable resources in the process! How do you approach your intended audience? If they are truly integral to your cause, understanding what's important to them will help shape your marketing plan. ("Do better at doing good" Harvard Business Review, May 1996)

Value Proposition:

A value proposition accomplishes two strategic objectives: Defines what your organization can do better than anyone else (competition) and secondly, why that's important to your audience. If your mission/vision statement is not clear on that point, how can the rest of your organization and audience feel the same way? In the Land of Oz, the Wizard had a very clear and powerful value proposition despite the fact that he couldn't deliver on his promises.

Al Ries and Jack Trout, noted marketing experts, said it best—"perceptions, not products" (Ries & Trout, 1994). This critical point of contention is often over-looked, or in the planning process, is written once and then set aside. The entire organization must be compelled by this "rallying cry" and live the brand promise each day! (Knapp, 2000)
The key to defining a value proposition is an arduous task and requires time, patience, and tenacity on the part of management. One organization I researched had a lingering problem—the perception didn't match what they actually did. Although their mission, philosophy, and business plan reflected one set of attributes, the brand perception unveiled in audience surveys revealed a very different perception. Does your collateral material mirror what you do?

Marketing Public Relations:

The most widely ignored marketing tool available to all organizations is public relations (Harris, 1999). Great companies like Starbucks™ and The Body Shop™ were built on public relations and only used advertising later on to support/update their message. The Wicked Witch of the East made personal appearances throughout the story to ingrain her message into the frightened travelers. The Witch's compelling message was looming and ubiquitous. Is your organization's message compelling and meaningful?

For-profits rely on purchased mediums as their message generator and issue press releases as an afterthought. Most nonprofits utilize volunteers or "friends" who can acquire an occasional story in the local paper or regional magazine. You can follow the yellow brick road and stick with traditional media or seek out the places where your targeted audience works/plays. The shear number of free placements in highly segmented forums is astounding. Internet portals that deal with your for-profit/nonprofit issues are numerous and seek a continuous stream of articles to support their sites. Other than the obvious regional and local papers, a variety of more niche publications will gladly give you space to tout your message. If scarce monetary resources are one of your most challenging dilemmas, let marketing public relations provide a venue to achieve your goal at minimal expense. Also keep in mind that third party editorials (PR), according to Theodore Levitt of Harvard Business School, are the most credible messages (Levitt, 1997).

Messaging:

Dorothy had an unmistakable message throughout her journey—I want to go home! Every action she took and anyone who would lend an ear heard her specific cause. What is yours? Every aspect of your messaging, both visual and intangible, should specifically point to that mantra. When you think of Overnight Package Delivery, does Fed Ex™ come to mind? What about "The Ultimate Driving Machine?" Does BMW™ sound familiar? How about "Just Do It?" Try Nike™.

The human mind can only attach one specific meaning or feeling to each item. Although a brand represents a culmination of all attributes, we really only remember one distinct thing. Let's start with your logo and by-line (sometimes called tag line). A by-line should be both emotional and descriptive (Schmitt/Simonson, 1998). Going back to our BMW™ example, "ultimate" is an emotional aspect and "driving machine" is the descriptive. Does your by-line capture the essence of your value proposition? Does it instantly tell your potential audience who you are and your compelling story?

The by-product of your messaging should generate passion and action. Dorothy convinced the Scarecrow, Tin Man, and Cowardly Lion to journey to Oz based on a compelling value proposition (brand promise). Most messages are directed at attributes and correlate cause to effect. This approach lacks inspiration and polarizes the recipient. Does your message invoke passion and action?

Simply put, every message you produce (business cards, newsletters, website, etc.) culminates into a single, brand position. Each additional layer of messages you generate are either acknowledged or disregarded by this audience based on your original pronouncement. Be mindful of the context and character your organization delivers. Is your message as clear and compelling as Dorothy's?

MARKETING EXERCISES

Marketing Plan: A marketing plan should stipulate five basic concepts:

1. The current business landscape you operate in

2. Situational analysis (self-evaluation)

3. Who you are and what value you provide

4. Targeted audience and channel to market

5. Promotional venue to achieve your objectives

Most bookstores carry a variety of material that outlines a marketing plan and guides you through the process. To make things easier, most books contain a computer program which prompts you fill in the necessary information. What's important here is the content and point-of-view. As noted on page 13, the approach you take to market will have a significant impact on whether you penetrate the "minds" of your intended audience.

The key to a successful marketing plan is to discern important issues facing your target market (landscape). If you feed the hungry, then knowing why your intended audience would give to your cause reins supreme. If gratification in helping others drives their behavior, then the focus of your message should center on that one issue. This outside-in approach of starting with your audience and working back to what your organization injects significant meaning into the value proposition. In this manner, you are addressing what is important to your audience, then providing them a venue to exercise that behavior.

Value Proposition: As noted above, a value proposition accomplishes two strategic objectives: Defines what your organization can do better than anyone else and secondly, why that's important to your audience. This strategic task takes time and diligence to define, articulate, and congeal into a deliverable that the masses can easily consume. In addition to developing this message, you must take every opportunity to pronounce the virtues of it on a continuous basis. This proposition begins within the organization, and through messaging, flows to the intended audience.

Try this exercise. Approach two or more of your senior managers and ask them, in one sentence, to define your value proposition (what you do better and why that's important). If you get an array of divergent responses, it's time to re-align your mission statement and then infuse those beliefs into the organization.

The essence of a value proposition can be seen at your local fast food restaurant. Although you may take it for granted, every aspect of what you see, hear, smell, taste, and feel was strategically designed and executed. Travel to another city and that value proposition will once again be presented in meticulous detail. Why should your organization be any different? A value proposition doesn't transpire through osmosis.

<u>Write below your value proposition:</u>

_____

What can your organization do better than anyone else?

_____

Why would that be important to your audience?

(We will use your value proposition later in the workbook)

Marketing Public Relations (MPR): The most ignored tool in an organization's toolbox is public relations. As you well know, PR enables entities to freely publicize their activities at no cost (other than writing the piece). The essence of MPR has more to do with strategy than the actual editorial you see in a publication. Take "The Body Shop™" example. Anita Roddick started her little shop without the use of advertising. Her value proposition was "environmentally responsible makeup for women" and she touted her message to anyone that would listen. She proclaimed her cosmetics were free of animal testing and they were purchased from third-world countries (helped the under-privileged economy). This Eco-message played well in the press and she ascertained millions of dollars of free press in the process.

What about your cause? What compelling message or story needs to be touted to the press? List below a few potential headlines that encapsulate your value proposition and would be interesting for general consumption?

Compelling message #1

_____

Compelling message #2

_____

If you are like most organizations, you have limited funds available to get your message out. Instead of spending precious dollars on advertising, utilize your internal talented writers to generate interesting stories about your cause. Next, submit them to the press, but more importantly, find local papers, magazines, and web sites that speak to the audience you are seeking. In most cases, these publications need content and are more than likely to give you space in their venue. It really comes down to effort: how persistent and committed you are to "getting the word out" will define your success rate. Also, make sure you clip those articles and ask the publisher (or acquire their ad rate card) how much it would cost to run the same piece if you paid for it. Next, keep track of the number of free press that ran and the associated cost (savings). By year-end, you should have accumulated hundreds, if not thousands of dollars in free press!

Messaging: The essence of messaging is a culmination of everything you generate as an organization over time and becomes the reality in each individual's minds-eye! What exactly does that mean? Think of McDonald's™ Restaurant. Everything you see, hear, smell, taste, feel, and think about this operation comes from years of messaging. Billboards, TV ads, newspapers, magazines, the golden arches sign, and many other symbols, jingles, etc., come together to form a single impression in your mind. That single impression will determine whether your audience will choose you or other offerings on any given day.

Now let's turn to your by-line (sometimes referred to a tag-line). If "Just do it" is Nike™, then what message embodies your organization? The importance of a by-line is it instantly informs the audience of your value. Back to the BMW™ example, Ultimate (emotional) Driving Machine (functional) describes it all! Does your by-line combine an emotional and functional message that invokes passion and action to your cause? If it is boring and lifeless after you read it, think about how your audience feels? Remember, people want to be associated to things that inspire and have meaning. Why else would you pay $150 for a pair of running shoes unless it processed a familiar symbol that told the world…"Hey, I wear Nike shoes."

Describe below your current and future by-line. After writing these down, determine why one would be more meaningful than the other to your audience?

<u>Current By-line</u>   <u>Future By-line</u>

_____   _____

Finally, make sure all facets of your organization are consistent. Every written word such as business cards, web site, form letters, building sign, etc., must reflect this consistent message. If your new by-line appears one place but not the other, you'll only create confusion.

<u>Summary:</u>

This section addressed several key aspects of marketing. A plan should center on customer circumstances and use public relations, a unique value proposition, and the appropriate messaging to capture the consumer's heart and mind. Using the analogy of Dorothy and her journey, we are reminded that a consistent and pervasive message should permeate every facet of your organization. In addition, all messaging should inspire your customer base to join your journey.

Market Analysis

I attended a lecture series at Oxford University and one presenter, Dr. Richard Schoenberg, illustrated why some organizations succeed while others fail to harness the essence of customer satisfaction. His concept could be applied to any ongoing concern and quickly depicts gaps between products/services offered and actual consumer behavior. Several months later I came across another body of research that dealt with similar issues, but the model and approach differed. Dr. Clayton Christensen (Harvard Business School) proposed his theory that unveiled the difference between innovative verses a sustaining business model and the process of emergent verses deliberate strategies. A myriad of other relevant concepts from accomplished authors were also applied to this section to complete the discussion of market analysis.

The following "meta-analysis" (culmination of works) illuminates and discusses the essentials of several academic theories and compares/contrasts them to an archetypal, organization. The assumption is that most entities utilize flat organizations and their budgetary constraints limit access to consultants who can acquire and apply such concepts. Furthermore, fulfilling their daily challenges affords little time to reflect on strategic shifts in their value segment. This brief alerts senior management to contemplate these theories and to assess applicability to their own organizational design. The following FOUR steps will help the organization's management apply these concepts to their own business.

Step1: Defining Business Model Type

Organizations tend to define WHO they are and WHAT they do based on the task at hand. For example, if you knit sweaters for the homeless, one might consider themselves "clothiers" and their goal is to clothe those in need. Another way to evaluate our example is based on disciplines and methods that constitute a business model. To continue with our example, if one were to make the highest quality sweater, then they would be considered "best product" and the organizational attributes would be structured around that process (The Discipline of Market Leaders, Michael Treacy & Fred Wiersema). If you highly customize your sweaters, you would be considered "customer intimate" and if your organization was highly efficient at that process, you would be deemed "operationally excellent."

According to Treacy & Wiersema, all organizations operate in all three arenas simultaneously, but the entity is organized around one dominate process. By stepping back and considering these two strategic issues, mainly WHAT you do and HOW you do it, you can quickly identify your business model type. This determination, in my opinion, is critical when undertaking a value-gap analysis.

Step 2: Value-Gap Analysis

The framework of a value-gap analysis is comprised of two constituencies: identification of gaps in consumer value that are not being fulfilled and re-defining the competitive rules. Let's look at an organization in a business that most of us are familiar with—the airline industry. Back in the 1980's, Southwest Airlines™ found a gap (low-cost, no frills travel) in the airline industry and built a business model around that unfulfilled need. Management understood that competing head-to-head (using their rules) of the other giant airlines meant certain disaster. Southwest Airlines™, in effect, changed the rules and was rewarded with market dominance and monetary prosperity during tumultuous times. Southwest built a low-cost business model by employing point-to-point service, using one aircraft type (Boeing 737) that reduced maintenance costs, and cross-functionally trained all their employees to engage in multiple activities.

A value gap analysis consists of plotting your direct competitors on at least seven key attributes they consistently deliver. Next, by observing behavior or through surveys, have your target audience rate each attribute in terms of importance. The variance between competitive offerings and customer behavior will readily emerge. By reducing, eliminating, or increasing those attributes, a new position will be created that more accurately portrays the behavior of your targeted audience. This exercise not only identifies opportunities, but also reduces or eliminates activities that consumers do not value and in turn, reduces associated costs.

If we apply this theory to the Southwest™ example (see graph), one can quickly assimilate attributes of importance to the discount traveler and by filling those needs, how a successful business might be developed. As this

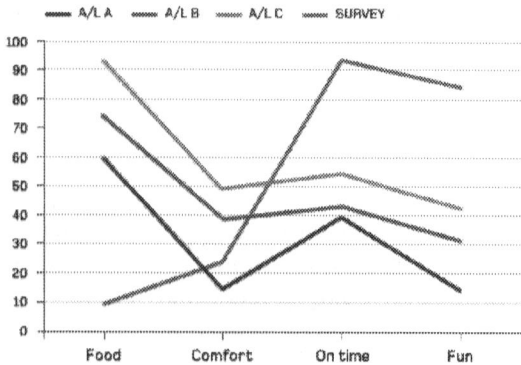

graph indicates, customers felt that food and comfort, which airlines were offering, possessed little value when compared to on-time flights and a fun experience. As a result, Southwest™ eliminated meals, minimized seating, focused on frequency of on-time flights, and created a "fun" experience from check-in to the final destination.

To summarize, Dr. Richard Schoenberg suggests mapping the behavior of your target audience and finding "gaps" that are being ignored or underdeveloped. Next, adjust your business model to eliminate, reduce, or increase value in areas that are meaningful to the user. Finally, change the rules of the game and make them hard to follow.

Step 3: Sustaining verses Disruptive Business

Another approach to assessing the marketplace for your organization considers circumstances over generally accepted quantitative tools/methods for creating growth. Let's start with how the organization categorizes its business.

According to Christensen, people "hire products to do specific jobs in everyday matters (The Innovator's Solution, Christensen)." Most professional organizations utilize market research personnel or firms to quantitatively analyze the "numbers" and derive correlations between attributes and customers. Christensen suggests that "the functional, emotional, and social dimensions of the jobs that customers need to get done constitute the circumstances in which they buy." The critical point here is that segmenting your business around circumstances, verses customers, will determine your success. Returning to the Southwest™ example, the circumstances of discount and business flyers warranted a demand for inexpensive, high frequency, and fun travel. The Southwest™ business model embodied functional (frequency/inexpensive), emotional (fun/relaxing), and social (light-hearted service, whimsical) with every experience. In short, Southwest™ segmented their business along the circumstances of travel and not the customer and has built a 34 year history of success.

Christensen asserts three approaches to creating growth: sustaining, low-end disruptions, and new market disruptions. What is the importance of these concepts to nonprofits or any other organization? The unequivocal answer is all organizations need to grow! By now, you have discerned WHO and WHAT your organization does and whether the dominant process entails best offering, customer intimacy, or organizational competence. Next, you undertook a value-gap analysis and determined gaps and considered shifting the rules of competition. Also, you've considered the circumstances as to WHY people buy and how they hire products/services to achieve them.

The next step involves how you are going to create growth. A sustaining approach seeks to continuously improve the offering and initiate cost containment. A second approach is deemed a low-end disruption (ex. Southwest Airlines™) that delivers "good-enough" performance at affordable prices. The final, or new market disruption, competes against non-competition. (The depth and complexity of this topic could not be contained in this chapter and the author recommends reading Christensen's book.)

The importance of which growth strategy you select solidifies the direction and actions you'll take. If your organization continuously improves its methods to deliver a service while clamping down on costs, the path taken equates to a sustaining strategy, which increasingly adds more performance to capture growth. If the increasing capability exceeds what customer's desire (over-shoot needs), the possibility exists for a segment of consumers to seek other venues. An example might be a grass-roots organization that, over time, has taken on too many causes in an effort to grow. In this case, consumers might feel the message has been diluted and will find another cause to support (one that is more focused).

Step 4: Deliberate verses Emergent Strategies

A final theory posed by Christensen culminates with WHAT you do and HOW you do it in relation to the marketplace and your organization on the whole. He suggests that two simultaneous processes operate in every organization that defines strategy. A "deliberate" strategy is derived by analysis, is measurable, and is implemented by senior management. An "emergent strategy" is derived from unanticipated opportunities and is a process of daily decisions of the organization.

Let's go back to our sweater business example. You make two sweaters—one is made out of cotton and the other wool. Your strategic direction is to donate the more durable sweaters next year, but the organization receives requests for the cheaper, cotton sweaters. Thus, the organization allocates resources to invest in cotton material and the net result is the organization's actual strategy. Herein lies a crucial question—do you adapt emergent opportunities/problems or force a deliberate strategy on your organization?

MARKET ANALYSIS EXERCISES

Defining Business Model Type: All businesses operate in all three models, but the organization clearly distinguishes itself by specific attributes. As noted above, an organization can be best product, customer intimate, or operationally excellent. Which one are you?

To undertake this exercise in depth, my recommendation would be to read Michael Treacy and Fred Wiersema's book "The Discipline of Market Leaders." A brief snap-shot of the three models derived from Treacy & Wiersema's book enables the reader to choose the one that best reflects their current behavior:

Product Leadership:

Culture: Concept, future driven, experimental
Organization: Ad-hoc, organic, and cellar

Customer Intimate:

Culture: Client focused and field driven
Organization: Entrepreneurial client teams

Operational Excellence:

Disciplined teamwork, process focused
Organization: Centralized functions, high skills at core

Please list below your current model and a desired direction.

_____   _____

            Current   Desired

Why is this exercise important? The point of contention lies in the realm of "organizational schizophrenia." Management may view the operation in one regard, but in actuality, it really operates in a completely different fashion. One firm I worked with operated as "customer intimate," but "product leadership" drove another portion of the business. In effect, every aspect of the business was torn (resource allocation, human capital, messaging, etc.) in two very different directions.

To undertake an organizational analysis, you must consider every aspect of your current design and operating protocol at each level. All too often, management espouses a plan and assumes the organization will readily adopt and act on that premise. In actuality, humans operate on survival instincts and tend to behave in a manner that's contrary to "the plan." We will discuss deliberate verses emergent strategies later in this section.

The take-away from this exercise is to crystallize one dominant business model. This must be accomplished before we move on to the value-gap analysis. In summary, your capacity to evaluate this gap is subject to a definitive business model and organizational behavior.

Value-Gap Analysis: As noted on page 21, a Value-Gap analysis merely identifies the attributes your target audience highly values and plots them on a graph. By listing those attributes along the X-axis and level of importance along the Y-axis, you can quickly plot the salience of each attribute accordingly. Several opportunities will quickly emerge.

The starting point to this exercise resides in the area of qualitative research: focus groups or customer surveys are preferred over statistical (quantitative) methods since you are not seeking Yes or NO answers to your questions. The key to undertaking qualitative research lies in the approach.

Meaningful information delves into the behavioral aspects of your audience. Referring back to the Southwest™ example on page 22, you are seeking the reason why your audience finds little value in airline food. Conversely, asking your audience "would you like food served on a flight," most respondents would reply "yes." If you pursued that line of questioning a little further, you would unveil that this audience prefers not to eat on short flights and/or prefers to pick something up along the way. The challenge to any survey seeks the motive behind the behavior.

Using the graph below, label and plot (use a red marker) the five attributes that your research indicates is highly valued by your audience. On a scale of zero to one (one being highly valued), plot the aggregate responses:

Value-Gap Chart

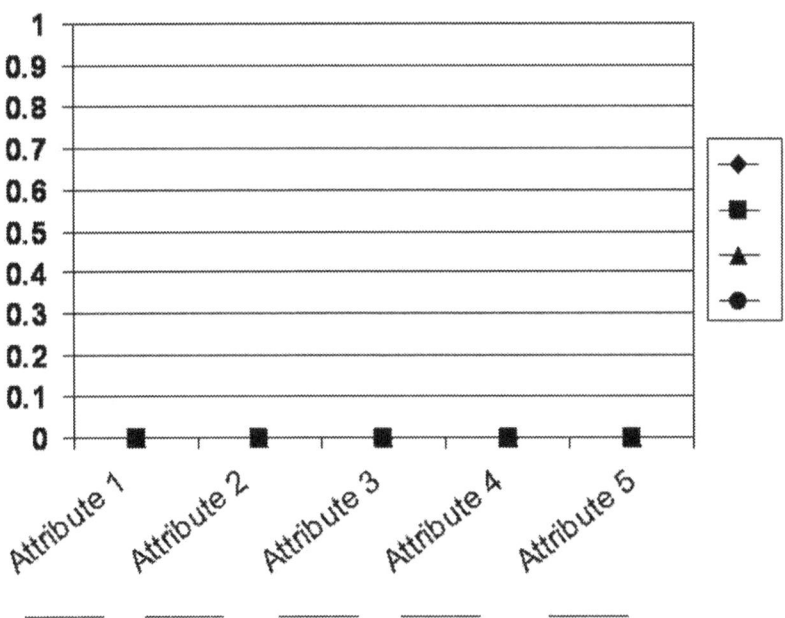

Next, list two competitors and graph their attributes on the above chart (use yellow and green markers). Finally, indicate your performance by graphing (in blue) the value you deliver for each attribute. Compare and contrast what your audience values (red) compared to what you and your competitors deliver. At this point, it should be clear which gaps in value exist.

Identify areas that your audience deems as little value and consider this as an opportunity to reduce or eliminate that particular attribute. In areas where you and your competitors are not actively addressing, increase your offerings to meet their expectations. In effect, this exercise will guide your adjustment of your business model to meet the behavioral activities of your target audience.

The importance of a Value-Gap analysis is two-fold: find opportunities that are not being addressed and secondly, change your business model to be more efficient at delivering the kind of value that a specific audience deems important. All organizations have thin resources—why squander them on activities that possess little or no value to them?

Sustaining verses Disruptive Business: As noted on page 22, the next step involves how you are going to create growth. A sustaining approach seeks to continuously improve the offering and initiate cost containment. A second approach is deemed a low-end disruption that delivers "good-enough" performance at affordable prices. The final, or new market disruption, competes against non-competition. Every organization needs to challenge its core premise and assess which of the three best represents their daily activities.

Which one are you? Answer these two questions. First, does your organization continuously improve its offerings (sustain) or disrupts the status quo in your market segment?

_____

Sustain or Disrupt?

Secondly, if your organization disrupts, do you provide "good enough" features or compete against ideas, values, or concepts that don't exist?

_____

Low-end disrupt or compete against non-competition?

The importance of answering this question directly influences the trajectory you will take in the future. For example, if you sustain (improving while cutting costs), eventually some other organization will find a better approach or more efficient method than the one you operate under today. Back to the airline industry, low cost carriers are profitable while most of the major carriers wallow in chapter 11 (low-end disruption). For your consideration: re-evaluate the competitive nature of your market space annually, and at the same time, determine which of the three forces are taking shape and by whom.

Deliberate vs. Emergent: As noted on page 29, there resides a simultaneous process that operates in every organization that defines strategy. A "deliberate" strategy is derived by analysis, is measurable, and is implemented by senior management. An "emergent strategy" is derived from unanticipated opportunities and is a process of daily decisions by the organization.

Most leaders believe that when they establish a strategy for next year the organization merely implements it. This premise remains true, given management's diligent efforts to continuously drive these initiatives. However, an underlying event occurs at the same time that also drives strategy which evolves from outside of the firm. Citing a previous example, let's say you produce wool sweaters for the homeless. The local shelters begin to request cotton sweaters instead and soon you will need to adapt to the emergent needs and adjust (purchases, processes, etc.) accordingly. Unless management steps in (to their detriment) and takes a deliberate action to continue making wool sweaters, cotton sweaters will prevail.

How is your strategy formulated? Please note below.

_____

Deliberate or Emergent?

What forces (outside-in) are affecting your strategy?

_____

Political, environmental, regulatory, competition, others?

Do you adapt to emergent forces or oppose them?

_____

One final note: be careful how you treat emergent forces on your organization—they may provide a glimpse into how your segment might be changing in the future!

Summary: The intent of this section was to introduce several market analysis theories and then generate reflection on the part of management. Most organizations stretch their thin resources to accomplish the task at hand without having to consider "competitive forces" which are lurking around the corner. Since time, money, and energy are limited commodities, the ability to think strategically about your organization's direction is more crucial than ever.

Undertaking a marketplace analysis achieves two strategic objectives: it identifies WHAT you do and HOW you do it with respect to the current circumstances of your target audience. A value-gap analysis quickly discerns those attributes that are important and which to increase, reduce, or completely eliminate. Also, are you attempting to sustain your current activities or create new value which will determine a future direction. Finally, will you follow the emergent opportunities or drive deliberate strategies to initiate growth. The answers to these questions will not only define your organization's future, but also re-organize how you serve your existing constituents.

BRAND TRAPS

If you search the term "branding" on the Internet, you'll be inundated by a plethora of theories, assumptions, and case studies which implicate the quintessential approach to this elusive topic. This mystification leads most organizations to relegate brand management to lower level functionaries and relies on tangibles, such as revenues and EBITDA, as a measure of market viability.

The strategic use of branding typically surfaces when the organization experiences a turbulent period in time. Brand principles are then misapplied as a life preserver. Have you ever noticed organizations that are floundering and are heading for certain disaster? Tall tale signs are the over use of branding tactics as a means to change perception. They are desperately trying to tell you that things are "ok."

The fundamental problem with the application of branding lies in its strategic importance and execution throughout the organization. If top management views branding as a "marketing function," their cursory involvement implicates a tactical view and permeation throughout the organization will not congeal. What arises is a PHANTOM BRAND—one that exists in the murky shadows and becomes a vague reminder of an organization's true self. Conversely, an organization that embraces their brand as the strategic cornerstone of the business and obtains cultural acceptance will emerge with a strong identity and market position.

The intent of this section is to identify brand traps and understand why they fall into disrepair. Published authors' who have investigated various facets of this topic will be cited and their findings summarized. The by-product of this exercise will alert management to patterns and red flags that signify brand dilution.

Branding Defined:

Many specialists have defined branding over the years. Michael Dunn, CEO of Prophet Consulting, states, "the brand acts as a sort of shorthand that consumers use to decide between competing products." In the broadest sense, the brand is a combination of a product or services' public image. Another branding expert of 31 years broke the concept down into 22 Immutable Laws of Branding (Al & Laura Ries, 2002) in which law number five deals with brand ownership. They assert, "if you want to build a brand, you must focus your branding efforts on establishing a word in the prospect's mind—a word that nobody else owns." Finally, David Aaker, noted expert on brand strategy states, "a company's brand is the primary source of its competitive advantage and a valuable strategic asset (Building Strong Brands, 1996)." Now that branding has been defined, let's examine common foibles of brand management.

Common Branding Traps:

David Aaker has identified four brand identity traps that can lead to ineffective and dysfunctional brand strategies. These "traps" include image, position, external perspective, and product-attribute fixation traps. Aaker contends that a brand image reflects the past and is passive in nature, whereas the brand identity is active and focuses on the future. Let's briefly review Aaker's brand trap theories.

1. Brand Image Trap:

The essence of this first trap is how customers perceive your brand image. If left un-checked, the brand image slowly becomes the brand identity. The problem here is that both the customer and the marketplace are defining your identity verses the company creating a more accurate portrayal of your future brand promise.

2. Brand Position Trap:

A brand position utilizes the value proposition to actively communicate and demonstrate its brand advantage in the marketplace. The trap occurs when the focus is on product attributes rather than brand building activities (personality, associations, symbols, etc.). As a result, the brand lacks depth and significance and could be equated to a movie with a weak plot—dull and uneventful!

3. External Perspective Trap

The common viewpoint of organizations is to maintain an external focus—how customers perceive the brand. Most organizations fail to internally communicate the vision and values of their brand. Test this concept yourself: Ask anyone within your organization what your brand stands for—if you get a blank stare or a numerical response (in the form of a sales goal), then you've got issues. How can your employees execute the brand promise to your customers if they lack passion, inspiration, and understanding?

4. Product-Attribute Fixation Trap

The failure to distinguish between a product and a brand is the essence of a product-attribute trap. Most companies view product attributes as the basis for purchasing decisions and competitive strength in the marketplace. Although Nike™ produces professional quality running shoes (as does others), the identity-association of owning the product has greater meaning to the owner than the product itself. Ask someone what they drive? If they possess a sense of pride, they'll quickly respond with the brand name—not horsepower or torque ratios!

What Aaker proposes are common brand traps that organizations intentionally or unintentionally drift into over time. This insight will help marketing practitioners consider their current methods and help avoid commonplace foibles.

New Brand or Position:

Al Ries recently discussed three mistakes companies make when launching new products (or brands) in the marketplace. The first common mistake is to spend big during the initial roll-out. The reasoning is—if they don't know you're there, they won't buy! According to Ries, new products (brands) take off slowly and advertising inherently lacks credibility. Successful organizations have built their brand solely by utilizing public relations (such as The Body Shop™, Swatch™, and Red Bull™).

The second mistake, according to Reis, is using a research-driven name. The biggest brand name in online book sales is Amazon.Com™, not "Bookfinder.com." Why? History has demonstrated that consumers seek differentiated identities online and organizations such as pets.com and etoys.com (generic) have also failed.

The third mistake Ries states is broad distribution. Whether it is the placement of products or advertising to launch a new name/product, Ries suggests that you start small. When you narrow your focus and concentrate on one method (market, distribution point, etc.), your brand has a better chance of being recognized verses being lost amongst the giants in the same environment.

Phantom Brands:

Author Matt Haig suggests "consumers make buying decisions based around the perception of the brand rather than the reality of the product (Brand Failures, 2003)." He goes on to say that the value extends beyond the physical assets of the organization and that perception is fragile at best. (His work exemplifies those entities that discarded the immutable laws of branding and suffered the inevitable consequences). The following excerpts from Haig's book "Brand Failures" demonstrate how organizations ignored the strategic importance of their most valuable assets:

Snapple™: Beverages

Quaker Oats Company bought Snapple™ for $1.7 billion in 1994 and decided to change the brand formula. They shifted its distribution and advertising campaign to reflect something that it wasn't, and within three years, sold the floundering company for $300 million. The lesson learned? Quaker Oats didn't understand the brand's value, both in place and presentation, and diminished the value in the consumer's mind.

Planet Hollywood™: Restaurant

Most of us have "tried" Planet Hollywood and enjoyed the novelty of the experience. This organization was launched in 1991 with the premise of celebrity hype and movie memorabilia, with food being a sideline. By 1999, the company went bankrupt and its fortunes invested lost. What happened? Since the "food" wasn't the reason to visit Planet Hollywood, once you've seen the sights, there was no compelling reason to return.

McDonald's Arch Deluxe™: International Chain

The tag line for this product was "Burger with a grown-up taste" it was McDonald's biggest flop. The value proposition for this organization is friendliness, cleanliness, consistency, and convenience. The product concept was well researched and the consensus was positive. Why did Arch Deluxe fail? McDonald's ignored their values and offered a more affluent product that didn't match their brand identity. Market research should be considered as input, but if it denies your brand, put little trust into it!

Phantom brands arrive at our doorstep in many forms. For some, a serious lack of brand management allows the organization's most valuable asset (the brand identity) to erode over time and become less valuable to their customers. For others, a deliberate act (Snapple) for profit's sake quickly destroys the point of differentiation in the consumer's minds. Phantom brands become remnants of an organization's true value/inspiration and quickly drive the organization into disrepair. Why does this occur?

In my experience, the problem lies squarely with senior management and their incomprehension of the brand concept. The spotlight shines on revenues and relationships, which is the fuel of business, but the engine remains the brand. As a result, they miss the warning signals and unconsciously make decisions that ultimately diminish the organization's value. Since the CEO is typically the chief marketing officer, it is his or her responsibility to care and nurture their brand identity. Without such awareness, the dark shadows of mediocrity slowly engulf the brand and tarnish its very soul.

BRAND TRAPS EXERCISES

The marketing function usually resides in the hands of those with minimal experience or strategic oversight. If your first reaction is disbelief, then visit a few firms and ask "who" in the organization is making critical branding decisions. What you'll quickly find out is a VP holds the official title, but a lower level manager makes the daily decisions. If you dig a little deeper, those who care for the brand usually lack a formal education in marketing and have not invested in current articles or books on the subject. What's wrong with this picture?

There resides, in my opinion, a dis-connect between leaders who create and guide strategic decisions and those who communicate the message. Since leaders put little stock in the marketing function, the potentially valuable asset becomes an afterthought. Until such time that leaders embrace brand management and elevate it to a leading strategic function, ensuing brand traps may falter the organizations future goals. Let's examine a few of these traps.

Brand Image Trap:

The essence of this first trap is how customers perceive your brand image. Please note your preferred identity on the left and then ask audience members how you are perceived.

_____	_____
Preferred Identity	How your audience/marketplace defines you

If you repeat this process several times, by asking members of your organization and audience to respond, you'll be surprised by the contrast between the two.

Brand Position Trap: A brand position utilizes the value proposition to actively communicate and demonstrate its brand advantage in the marketplace. The trap occurs when the focus is on product attributes rather than brand building activities (personality, associations, symbols, etc.).

What type of brand building activities are you engaged in on a daily basis? Are those activities centered on features and benefits or the development of brand personality? List three activities your organization engages in to develop your brand identity:

1. To build personality? _____
2. Build associations? _____
3. Create symbols? _____

The essence of this exercise is to explore story-building elements of your brand. What is the difference between a uneventful and a great book, between a poor or a captivating movie? The storyline your organization creates and nurtures will become the basis by which your audience recalls and appreciates what you do. Merely focusing on your attributes will not engender a passion for your cause.

External Perspective Trap: The discussion thus far has centered on external branding. What about the internal audience? As obvious as it may sound, many organizations take for granted that their vision and mission statements are fully understood. In addition, the desired change in behavior has been viewed as homogenous: by pronouncement, the organization would adapt and act accordingly.

Just like any well-nurtured and developed brand, an organizational adoption takes the same kind of patience and tenacity to properly infuse these messages and orientation. The next time you walk into a Starbucks™, pause to consider the orchestration of aesthetics and human capital. This seamless integration was artistically designed, developed, and executed to deliver an experience that fulfills the expectations and desires of the human experience.

Another prime example is the global Disney™ theme parks. Whether you are in Orlando, Anaheim, Paris, Tokyo, or Hong Kong, the "Magic Kingdom" delivers the same experience: organizational dress, behavioral, auditory—which equates to the "Disney Spirit." In the same manner, does your organizational behavior mirror what's written in your marketing or brand position plans?

Write below three of the activities you engage in on a monthly basis to infuse your vision and mission statement?

1. _____

2. _____

3. _____

The Starbucks™ and Disney™ examples are well planned and executed internal brand communications. They ignite the passion and essence of the brand and these employees "live" the promise daily. I should know—I was once a Disneyland tour guide during college and the training, attire, script, and mannerisms were well crafted and executed.

Product-Attribute Fixation Trap

The failure to distinguish between a product and a brand is the essence of a product-attribute trap. Most companies view product attributes as the basis for purchasing decisions and competitive strength in the marketplace. What does this mean? Simply put, the identity-association of owning the product has greater meaning to the owner than the product itself.

For example, if you provide wool sweaters to the homeless, you probably want donors to think about the greater cause than the physical product. Why is this important? People respond to the human condition much more than material things. I remember as a child watching the movie E.T. at the theatre and hearing the sobs around me when this alien was departing earth in the final scene. Even though everyone knew it was just a movie and E.T. was really a puppet, we collectively were inspired by the underlying story. Do you have a compelling message?

What is your identity-association?

_____

Whatever you do, remember that people invest in the human condition. In some respects, the benefit from being associated with your cause adds to their well-being. Have you ever spontaneously given money to someone in need? How did you feel afterwards? You probably felt a sense of pride, belonging, self-sacrifice, etc. that was greater than the amount you gave in dollars and cents.

New Brand or Position: When considering a new brand or position in the marketplace, the four P's (product, price, place, and promotion) come into play. Management must then strategize how to best use their limited resources to achieve their marketing objectives.

During the introductory phase, organizations tend to spend big to "get the message out." This short burst of energy may achieve some notice, but without a consistent level of exposure, the message soon fades. Additionally, a new brand or position takes time to develop in the audience's mind. How do you launch a new initiative?

Next, what name or brand do you apply to that initiative? How you label your brand or offering is critical relative to its acceptance. Do you apply a generic association to your cause or differentiate based on a brand promise? Ask yourself this question: what makes your cause different than other possible options? If five organizations are providing sweaters to the homeless, why does your cause have more meaning or provide a better solution. In the nonprofit world, donors are seeking accountability for their gifts and desire substance. Likewise, the consuming public demands quality and assurance over a given life span.

Finally, how broad the geographic terrain you attempt to garner should be narrow and focused. Any organization, no matter the vastness of resources, should start small and concentrate on a core audience. Returning to our sweater maker example, an organization may want to focus on a city-level scope first before attempting a regional/national approach. Building a core base allows the revenue stream to broaden and support a brand strategy on a larger scale. In this manner, you are not "biting off more than you can chew."

How do you approach a new brand or position as it relates to publicizing? Note your current method and an alternate approach based on the above discussion.

Current Method   New Approach

_____   _____   _____

Summary:

This discussion briefly covered what brands are, traps that organizations fall into, and common mistakes made when launching or re-branding products or services. Several companies were identified in addition to brand dilution errors that each had made. In most cases, brand management takes a back seat to top-line revenue and financial metrics. In the three examples provided above, management ignored the basics of branding and paid an exorbitant price for doing so.

BRAND METRICS

This section attempts to frame the discussion in terms that business leaders are most comfortable with. I believe a paradox exists in mainstream business where the brand concept has little or no credibility. If "financial metrics" are more palatable to organizational leaders, then let's translate branding into quantifiable terms (ROCI).

What is this paradox?:

As defined by Merriam-Webster dictionary, a paradox is an idea, thought, or accepted notion that may be contrary to the truth. In today's business environment, marketing plays a subservient role in crucial imperatives that drive strategic trajectories of organizations. The notion of branding, primarily viewed as a subset of marketing, receives even less attention.

The branding paradox, more specifically, is the link between branding and an organization's market value, but at the same time, is received amongst corporate America as unrelated. The brand paradox is further compounded by erroneous conceptions of what marketing is and the real impact it plays in business valuation. A quick test—why would you consider buying Nike™ shoes or invest in their stock? Because their P/E ratio is 20.3 or your overwhelming desire to associate with this brand identity?

Why does it occur?:

In my estimation, the prime reason for this widely accepted opinion is the absolute dependence on financial imperatives. When considering a stock purchase or a business relationship with another public company, most leaders immediately turn to the annual report, skim the statements, and calculate key ratios. In their viewpoint, the numbers (historic) dictate the health and proposed future trajectory of a given concern. Unfortunately, there isn't a line item in an organization's 10K statement for neither brand contributions nor valuation. We all agree that Coca Cola™ and Nike's™ most valuable asset is their brand mark, yet try to find a financial valuation on the income statement or balance sheet. Touché!

Translation in financial terms:

During graduate school, my professor introduced us to a new concept called Integrated Brand Communications (IBC). Until such time, Intergraded Marketing Communications was the latest rave amongst organizations as a means to unify their corporate brand messages. IBC, on the other hand, quantifies media expenditures and through a spreadsheet format, allows the leader to evaluate the return on investment. In addition, a direct link (for the first time) can be established between media expenditures and growth in revenues.

This causal relationship between media placement and ROI is rarely utilized due to thin resources and the breakneck speeds that most organizations traverse. Another significant paradox is this—organizations use financial results as the key metric of performance, yet forego this critical analysis and squander precious resources in the process. In my opinion, the application of IBC provides management accountability and tangible metrics to assess their strategic branding and marketing initiatives!

An abbreviated ROCI spreadsheet (see note below) provides the framework by which a financial assessment can be undertaken. The essence of this exercise is to establish the available market potential, the current income flow without communications, and the ensuing outflow by pursuing an investment in brand communications. If this methodology was followed in pursuant years, a true ROCI could be established and evaluated in quantifiable terms.

(A abbreviated spreadsheet inspired by Shultz & Barnes' textbook can be viewed by following this link www.ibranz.com/IBCsample.html)

How can one effect change?:

The application of IBC shifts marketing philosophy from that of *measuring awareness to one of targeting opportunity*. For the first time, it forces marketing to analyze the overall category potential (market leaders per segment) and determine through a targeted effort what a focused IBC program can yield. This process also allows the monitoring of current media spend to assess the ROI from year-to-year. Finally, leaders can now apply accountability to marketing budgets and evaluate the effectiveness of different programs. In a world driven by financial metrics, isn't it time to measure your marketing staff and subsequent programs?

BRAND METRICS EXERCISES

What metrics do you currently use to assess success in your marketing activities? List three metrics below:

1. _____

2. _____

3. _____

Step back and consider your responses. If your answers are general in nature (not financially-based) and non-specific to targeted segments, you may want to reconsider your marketing strategy. The crux of any marketing activity lies in the results yielded for a given effort. Advertising firms are quick to point to placements (paid) as the method for affirming your marketing plan. Public relations firms, on the other hand, will enlist the use of public-interest stories as a method to achieve awareness.

The question of WHO you are trying to inform and educate dictates the method and approach. If your core audiences are affluent, twenty to thirty-year-olds, the venue might reside in a combination of key web sites, life style magazines, and local events. By starting with their behavior first and working back to the medium will enable you to determine the most effective methods to communicate your brand promise.

Once you have established the best channels to market, the use of paid advertisements and public relations (free press) in concert with other internally generated methods should collectively achieve the stated objectives.

Once you have solidified your method and approach, go back and review "translation into financial terms" and follow the application prescribed there.
Rather than restating this point, you may want to read Shultz & Barnes book "Strategic Brand Communications Campaigns" to fully understand and appreciate their theory and application of this process. The benefit one could derive from this investment is financial accountability to your integrated brand communications.

Final thoughts:

If management hired one individual to implement IBC throughout the organization, the return on investment and increase in business opportunities could dwarf the monetary expenditure in less than one year.

If your organization had just one staff member responsible for the marketing function, the accountability realized in the short term could be dramatic. The application of IBC not only helps to identify the What and the Why of your current marketing programs, it quickly enables leaders to shift investments from underperforming programs to those with more attractive returns!

CONCLUSION

As noted in the introduction, the purpose of this workbook was to provide vital branding tools, demonstrate their application, and enable you to become a Brand Advocate. After reading and working through exercises in each section, let's now summarize our collective findings.

Transfer answers from each section into the following "Brand Strategy Guide." This template can now guide your strategic marketing and branding activities during subsequent planning meetings.

How to use this Brand Strategy Guide

When consulting with organizations, the application of a strategy tends to be the most difficult part of the process. The Brand Strategy Guide serves to supplement your overall business plan. What does this mean?

For example, let's start with the Branding Basics section. When crafting your next business plan, understanding your current perception (both internal & external) provides a base-line understanding of "WHO" you are and the "VALUE" you provide. By evaluating this one point, you may choose to re-position your organization's message or confirm the stated messages are correct. Whatever the outcome may be, the reflection and consideration exerted demonstrates a proactive managing and nurturing of your organization's most valuable asset. If you invest the same time and consideration into each question posed, the byproduct will generate a powerful brand strategy for your organization. You, in turn, will become your organization's true Brand Advocate!

BRAND STRATEGY GUIDE

Branding Basics:

Current Perception (You): _____

Colleague's Perception: _____

Why someone would do business with you?

Your Organization: _____

Competition: _____

Brand Perception: List top four descriptors

1._____ 2._____
3._____ 4._____

List current and future brand goal:

Current: _____ Future:_____

List bridge(s) that allows shift?_____

Approach to embedding brand message into hearts & minds?

1._____ 2._____

List your value proposition & importance to customers?

_____

What is your compelling story?

_____

Current and future by-line?

Current:_____ Future:_____

Define your business model type: check one

Product leadership: __ Customer Intimate:__ Operationally Excellent:__

Review Value-Gap Analysis (Pg.21): What attributes do you change?

Increase Value: _____

Decrease value: _____

Eliminate: _____

What does your growth model look like? Sustain or Disrupt?

How do you sustain?_____

How do you disrupt the marketplace?_____

Is your business strategy deliberate or emergent?

_____

Brand Image Trap:? How are you perceived?

Self:_____ Marketplace:_____

What financial metrics do you use to gauge effectiveness?

1._____ 2._____

Bibliography

Section One: Branding Basics

Ries, Al & Laura. "22 Immutable Laws of Branding: How to build a product or service into a World-Class brand. Harper Collins, 2002.

Section Two: Essentials of Branding

Slater, Robert. "Jack Welch and the GE Way." McGraw-Hill, 1999

Section Three: Marketing

Harvard Business Review. "Do better at doing Good." May 1996

Ries, Al, Trout, Jack. "22 Immutable Laws of Marketing," Harper Business, 1993

Knapp, Duane. "The Brand Mindset: Five Essential Strategies for Building Brand Advantage throughout Your Company." McGraw-Hill, 2000

Harris, Thomas. Value-Added Public Relations: The secret Weapon of integrated Marketing." McGraw-Hill, 1998

Levitt, Theodore. "The Marketing Imagination." The Free Press, 1986

Schmitt, Bernd, Simonson, Alex. "Marketing Aesthetics: The Strategic Management of Brands, Identity, and Image." The Free Press, 1997

Section Four: Market Analysis

Schoenberg, Richard. Senior lecturer of International Business Strategy. Lecture at University of Oxford, October, 2003. The Business School, Imperial College of London.

Christenson, Clayton. "The Innovators Solution: Creating and sustaining successful growth." Harvard Business School Publishing, 2003

Treacy, Michael. Wiersema, Fred. "The Discipline of Market Leaders." Perseus Books, 1995

Section Five: Brand Traps

Haig, Matt. "Brand Failures: The Truth about the 100 biggest branding mistakes of All Time." Kogan Page Pub., 2003
Dunn, Michael. www.Prophet.com
Ries, Al & Laura. "22 Immutable Laws of Branding: How to build a product or service into a World-Class brand. Harper Collins, 2002.
Aaker, David. "Building Strong Brands." The Free Press, 1996
Ries, Al. "Three Mistakes When Launching New Products. What's Working in Biz, www.ries.com

Section Six: Brand Metrics

Barnes, Beth. Shultz, Don. "Strategic Brand Communication Campaigns." NTC Business books, 1999.

978-0-595-37619-3
0-595-37619-3

www.ingramcontent.com/pod-product-compliance
Lightning Source LLC
Chambersburg PA
CBHW021037180526
45163CB00005B/2158